The Professional Risk Owners Handbook

By

John Lawson MSc MBCS

Table of Contents

The Professional Risk Owner's Handbook

All views expressed in this book are those of the author

Independently published

First edition published 2018 (Print and electronic)

© John Lawson, 2018 (Print and electronic)

ISBN: 9781980696872

'Let's be the best at everything that requires no talent'

Paul O'Connell,

Captain, British and Irish Lions Rugby Team

Australia 2013

Introduction

I am a bit of a rugby fan; hey, I'm Welsh what do you expect? In 2007, Warren Gatland was appointed head coach of the Welsh Team and since then (with a few notable exceptions) has presided over a golden period in Welsh Rugby. Gatland has enjoyed phenomenal success as head coach of both Wales and the British and Irish Lions, and is widely tipped to become head coach of the New Zealand All-Blacks in the not too distant future. But one of Gatland's enduring memories came from something he heard when he was touring Australia as head coach of the Lions squad in 2013. He was inspired by a quote from the then captain, the formidable Irish lock forward, Paul O'Connell when he told his team that he wanted them to be 'the best they could at everything that requires no talent'.

Not only has this stuck in Gatlan's mind, but mine too. What I think O'Connell was asking of his team was to do the basics and do them well, and that is the first thing I ask of my teams when it comes to work. And that is what this book is all about. This book takes risk ownership back to the fundamentals and builds it back up. Too often I have seen organisations with very impressive risk registers, accompanied by graphs, trend analyses, reports and all the hoohah to go with them. But when you strip it back, people still don't understand what it means to be the owner of the risk. They don't understand the decision making framework, or when and how they should escalate a risk. The risk register has become what my good friend Dr. Kevin Street called 'a tartan comfort blanket'.

This book aims to correct that and teach a whole generation of risk owners exactly what they need to know.

I have been involved in the risk management business for quite a few years now, and have been a risk manager for most of them. In the course of my various positions, I have come to know a great many risk managers in a wide variety of settings and disciplines. I have also had the privilege of working with and training other risk managers.

But do you know what the funny things is about risk managers?

When you boil it down, very few of them of my acquaintance, actually manage risks.

As Chief Risk Officer in a large public sector organisation, I am responsible for the risk management system across the whole organisation, but I am actually responsible for managing only one risk.

Other than this one, I had a number of actions for which I was responsible which were helping other people to manage their risks but those risks themselves were not mine to manage. If the worst had happened and the risk had been realised, whilst I may have been accountable if I had not delivered on the action, it was not my neck on the block if the organisation fell apart (unless of course it was because the risk management system which I had instigated had failed)!

Risks are managed by risk owners, who are the people who are responsible and accountable for the part of the business directly affected by the risk.

In developing the system, I reached the point where I needed to train risk owners in what their role was. As a key part of that I wanted to produce a guide to risk ownership that my students could take away with them.

What I wanted was a simple guide to risk ownership in its broadest sense for people who were not risk management professionals. I wanted to help people understand just what they were taking on when they became a risk owner; what it meant, what their responsibilities were, what limitations there were and how they could best discharge their duties as risk owners to the benefit of themselves, their organisations and their key stakeholders whether they be customers, service users or whoever.

This book is geared towards the system that I have put in place in several organisations both in the UK and Europe. That said, the system or a close variant of it is in widespread use throughout the world and so the principles and concepts discussed here could equally apply to a small business in Australia as well as a large public sector organisation in the UK.

This is not an academic text on risk management, there are plenty of those available from esteemed authors covering every aspect of risk from its history and origins right up to detailed studies of particular risk management techniques.

Neither will it explain how to manage particular types of risk. This book is not going to delve into the intricacies of health and safety management or financial or project risk. It isn't even aimed at risk management professionals who are managing and developing systems and to whom the fundamental principles laid out here should be very familiar

This book is intended as a short guide and is aimed at those people who have little or no experience or understanding of formal risk management in a business context and have either just been told that they are a risk owner, or have some nagging feeling that if something goes wrong it's them that will fall on the proverbial sword.

This book will provide a sound understanding of what it means to be a risk owner, regardless of the area of risk in which you are involved.

The fundamental principles of risk ownership outlined in this book will stand you in good stead regardless of what type of risk you are trying to deal with, whether it be financial, reputational, safety or anything else.

This then is a guidebook for risk owners. It will also prove useful to risk managers who are implementing and managing systems and want to have some clear direction as to what their risk owners can and cannot do.

Throughout the book I will refer to the system that I recommend because I have been using it for many years. Whilst most of the principles I discuss in this book are transferable regardless of the system, I would still recommend checking out within your organisation how their system works as you may see some differences.

How to use this book

I have tried to write the book in an easy going informal style in the same way that I deliver training on the same subject. If you so desire you can read the book in one sitting and get a broad appreciation of the topic, or if you already have some experience in the risk business, you may pick and choose your areas to concentrate on. Once you have covered what you need, the book is organised to provide a useful reference resource for the future. One thing I have done throughout the book is to highlight what in my experience are Key Points. These are highlighted at the end of each chapter and are provided for emphasis and to help guide those of you who have less time.

A word about Health and Safety

It is very important to emphasise the point here that this book discusses risk ownership in the context primarily of business risk where generally risk owners have more choice in what they do. In some cases however you have fewer choices and your actions could have legal implications. This is particularly notable in the field of Health and Safety risk where UK law requires that you manage risks down to a level which is 'as low as reasonably practicable'.[1]

You are advised therefore, that if you are responsible for risks involving the health and safety of any persons within your organisation you should consult a Health and Safety expert to ensure that you fully understand the implications of your actions.

---

[1] http://www.hse.gov.uk/Toolbox/managing/managingtherisks.htm (Accessed 1/3/18

Chapter 1

Risk fundamentals and the role of the risk owner

Let's be clear about something right from the start.

We are all expert risk owners. We have been doing it for a long time, ever since we came out of the cave and started to make our way to the click and collect point at Asda. An oft quoted definition of a risk is the potential for a hazard to cause harm. Think for a minute how many hazards you encounter every day from the moment you get out of bed and sometimes even before that.

The slippery shower tray, scalding hot water, an old bacteria-ridden toothbrush, the light-switch you operate with a wet hand, the dog running around your feet. These are just a few of the obvious hazards you face every morning before you even go downstairs.

Then there are the less obvious risks. The risk of not getting to your first meeting on time caused by the domestic emergency, or the risk of financial loss because of that credit card that keeps on slipping out of your worn out purse or wallet, and even the risk of reputational damage caused by choosing the wrong outfit.

So we are already experts in this stuff. Or are we?

The point is that we are all expert managers of risks that are familiar to us, risks that we have faced many, many times and have (almost) always managed successfully. We are experts in showering, we are experts on being punctual and whilst I am hardly a fashion icon, I do have a rough idea of which clothes will work and which will not.
And thereby lies the dichotomy; we struggle with risks where we are on unfamiliar territory or out of our comfort

zone, and we can become complacent with risks which we face every day. The risk owner then has a seemingly impossible job. But that is why I have written this guide, to help risk owners navigate these difficult waters and survive the journey.

So to go back to the risks on the previous page for a moment, what is it that they all have in common?

The answer is that we own them and by 'own' I mean that we can take responsibility for managing them. This doesn't necessarily mean that we can control them, at least not completely. What it means is that we have the power and authority to make decisions about them and are accountable for the consequences. We will talk a lot about decision making later in the book, but for now suffice to say that when it comes to risk management there are only 4 decisions you can take:

- You can terminate the risk
- You can transfer the risk
- You can treat the risk
- You can tolerate the risk

If and only if you have the power to make any of those decisions, then you can own the risk.

The important thing to remember here is not whether any course of action is acceptable or pleasant or even desirous, but that it is within your power to make should you choose to do so. By way of example, I would like to introduce you to Tom who is going to help me explain some key concepts throughout the book. It also introduces me to the first of my sketches. I could have called them examples I suppose, but I love sketching and I want to draw you a picture. So, let's go back to that slippery shower tray for a minute.

Sketch 1

Tom is a very image conscious sort of guy. He likes to shower and sort his hair out every morning without fail, before he goes to work or goes socialising. But Tom lives in a rented flat, and he has complained to his landlord several times about a worn and slippery shower tray and he thinks that there is a risk that he may fall in the shower and injure himself. As far as Tom is concerned, the shower belongs to the landlord, it isn't his responsibility to maintain it and so the risk belongs to the landlord and by telling him he has done all that he can to manage the risk.

Tom's reasoning is flawed however. He can and indeed does own the risk because he has the power to make decisions. He can terminate the risk by not using the shower. He doesn't find this acceptable as he doesn't want to smell bad, but he could choose this if he wanted to; it is within his power. He can treat the risk by paying out the money to have it replaced, but again he doesn't want to because he feels it is his landlord's responsibility to pay, not his. He can transfer some of the risk by buying insurance against personal injury again for which he would have to pay or he can simply tolerate the risk by accepting it for what it is and being a bit more careful, which is what he chooses to do.

Just to answer the question quickly, some of you may consider that Tom could escalate the risk to the landlord. We will revisit this in a later chapter and discuss why this simply doesn't work.

The landlord is of course also exposed to risk himself, but they are different risks, such as the financial and reputational risks involved if Tom has an accident and I'm not for one minute suggesting that Tom would have no recourse if he did slip. But that conversation is for a different book.

The role of the organisational risk owner

The risk owner's role is to take ownership of the risk on behalf of the organisation. But before we talk about what risk ownership entails, let's consider for a moment what risk ownership is not.

It is not about hierarchy.

Risk should always be owned and managed at the lowest available decision making level. So long as a person in an organisation has the authority to make the required decisions on a risk without referring upwards to another manager, then s/he should be capable of managing it.

It is a common misconception that risk owners need to be senior managers. Risk can be managed at any level of an organisation provided that the simple question of decision making authority has been answered. Even high risks can be managed at a relatively low level within an organisation provided this question is resolved.

In small businesses, there may only be one risk owner; sole traders are particularly notable in this aspect as there is no one else; the buck stops here!

It is not about location or convenience.

The risk owner should not be selected because they happen to work in the right place or department. The owner will not physically need to do all the controlling work on the risk as we shall see later, they just need to have access to the right people.

It's not even about control.

You can (and probably do) own risks which you cannot fully control. The lack of ability to control a risk is not a reason to say that you cannot own it.

Sketch 2
Tom like most people reads the newspapers and watches the television. He understands that however unlikely it may be, there is a risk that he will get caught up in a terrorist incident. This will be caused by him being in a crowded place at the wrong time and the impact would be...etc.

Now Tom can control the risk but only up to a point. He can transfer some of the risk by buying life insurance although it wouldn't benefit him personally very much. He can treat it by not going to anything that is considered high risk, and he can avoid big concerts and other high profile events. But realistically other than terminating the risk by deciding to go and live on a remote island somewhere (not realistic but nevertheless still possible and even then probably not a 100% guarantee) no matter what he does he can't completely avoid the risk. No one can completely avoid the possibility of getting caught up because there is no way of knowing where the terrorist will strike so whatever happens, Tom will end up tolerating the risk that remains. The risk is not fully within Tom's control but it is still Tom's to own however, because he can make any of the four decisions.

So what is it about then?

Risk ownership is about responsibility, accountability and above all about having the power to not only make decisions, but to turn those decisions into action.

Tom is starting to realise that the risk owner's chair can be a lonely place to sit sometimes so let's boil this down – as a risk owner, you are a gambler. You may be the sort of person who never buys a lottery ticket, you may never have bet on a horse and you wouldn't even think of walking into a betting shop. But as a risk owner you are a gambler, maybe even what the casinos in Las Vegas call a 'high roller'. You are gambling because risk is all about uncertainty and you are gambling on the likelihood and impact of a future event.

As the owner of a risk you have to take the decisions based on what you think is your estimate of the likelihood of a future event and how bad that event might be.

You could be gambling with the future of your organisation or you could be gambling with your personal assets and depending on your circumstances, you could even be gambling with people's lives.

The role of the owner takes in the whole lifecycle of a risk from initial identification through assessment, decision making, controlling, action planning and finally maintaining. We will discuss all these areas and more throughout this book.

The important thing when a new risk is identified is to establish from the start who the most appropriate owner could be. Risks will suddenly pop up in the strangest of places and the only person who knows anything about it could be quite low down in an organisation. It is very important therefore to find an appropriate owner as soon as possible to make sure that the right decisions are being made to manage the risk.

Key points

- *Risk ownership is gambling*
- *Risk ownership is about having the authority to make the decisions and turn decisions into action – it's not about control*

- *Just because a particular decision may be unpalatable does mean that it isn't yours to take*

Chapter 2

Risk Assessment Part 1

Definitions

Whilst this is not as I said in the introduction an academic work, we need to have a common understanding of some of the terms we are using. The definitions I put forward here are simple clear definitions to help people who are not risk professionals in gaining greater clarity on their roles.

Risk

It appears sometimes that there are as many different definitions of risk as there are risks that need managing. If you were to speak to people with different backgrounds, different perspectives or from different disciplines you would get many different answers to the question 'What is a risk?'.

To me, a risk needs to have some essential elements.

First, there needs to be an event that may or may not occur. This will be something measureable in the context of you can tell if it happens or not.

Secondly, the event will produce a negative outcome for the risk owner. This is an important point to stress, the negative outcome must be on the risk owner, or at least the risk owner's organisation. Now that might seem a little selfish, but run with me for now as we will come back to this point later. Now at this point I know that risk management professionals will all talk about opportunity risks as well, or good things happening. Opportunity risk is an important consideration, but in my experience this is usually dealt with during the planning phase of objective setting (for all risks must be linked to objectives as we will see later in this chapter), but for our purposes we are talking about risk in the negative sense, or of something going wrong.

Thirdly and arguably most importantly there must be a level of uncertainty surrounding the event. Without uncertainty there is no risk there is just a problem. I recall a discussion that I had with a senior manager some years ago where I was trying to explain this concept but he didn't quite get it and to emphasise his point he exclaimed *'Yes but there is a risk that I might die'.*

My response to this took him a little by surprise when I explained that he was wrong. There was no risk that he would die; that risk simply didn't exist. I could guarantee him, with 100% certainty that he would die. It wasn't a risk it was a fact. There was no uncertainty surrounding this at all. What I didn't know and where some uncertainty lay, was when, where and how it would happen (although by this point in the conversation I was prepared to speculate!)

Finally, there must be some likelihood of it actually happening, so we are not talking about theoretical or hypothetical risks here, there must be a degree of reality. In the case above, whilst theoretically possible I could say with some degree of certainty that this senior manager wouldn't die for example during a spacewalk, because he was not and never would be an astronaut. I could not say with any certainty however that it wouldn't happen when he crossed a busy road because he didn't check the traffic first. And that is where the real risks lay. To say there was a risk that he would die was missing the point and missing the risk.

Douglas Hubbard in his excellent book 'The Failure of Risk Management', takes those four elements and puts them into a simple definition with four simple words:

'Something bad might happen.'

From a point of view of operational risk management and particularly when trying to train non-professionals in how to manage risk, I have found this definition to be extremely helpful. All you need to do now, I tell my students, is to work out what is the 'something bad'.

Hazard or threat

Hazard or threat is a very good question. Those of you with some knowledge of Health and Safety will appreciate that identifying a hazard can be a pretty straightforward affair. The broken step tread, the blocked fire door or the unguarded machine are all easily identifiable hazards (at least to the trained eye). With business or corporate risk however the position is often more subtle or even nebulous and can take some pinning down.

Again in simple terms, a hazard or threat can be defined as:

'Something that has the potential to cause harm'

In this case the harm will probably not be to a person, but will more likely to be to the business or organisation, or more precisely will be harm to the objective against which the risk has been identified. This will sometimes take some thought; it will be almost like an itch that you can't quite reach, or the song you know so well but just can't remember the title.

We will talk later about the identification of threats and hazards.

Problems

So if what you are dealing with can't be defined as a risk or even a threat what will it be. The chances are that it's quite simply a problem and like any other problem it needs to be dealt with. How do you deal with a problem, well as there are as many solutions as there are problems, and that I'm afraid is beyond the scope of this book. The truth of the matter though is that the problem will almost certainly give rise to at least one risk if not more. The problem is usually a cause. If this is where you are with your description, you're going to need to go deeper.

Deciding which risks to worry about

Many more things in the world could happen than will happen. In other words there are literally millions of risks that we could choose to be concerned with, what we have to do first is to decide which ones are we going to try and manage and why. This requires us to take a long hard look at what we are trying to achieve; what are our objectives?

Risks need always to be tied closely to objectives, but this means that before we even start thinking about risks, we must be clear on what our objectives are. By far the clearest way of articulating your objectives is to make them SMART.
  * Specific
  * Measurable
  * Achievable
  * Realistic
  * Timescaled

A detailed study of SMART planning is beyond the scope of this book and there are any number of excellent management books available which will take you through the whole process of SMART objective setting. We will however revisit SMART in another context later on.

But to go back to the question, which risks should I worry about, well I'm afraid that no book is going to tell you that. It really is the $64,000 question. Only you and your organisation can decide which risks you want to worry about and which you don't, but if you follow the principles in this book you will have a pretty good idea where to start looking.

Think back a few pages to the argument I had with a senior manager when he told me that there was a risk that he might die. If you think about that for a moment, there is a myriad of ways in which I might die, and there are risks all around me that if they occurred could cause my death. How do I decide which ones to worry about and which to let go? It's simply a matter of personal choice. There is a risk that I could die in a meteor strike. There is very little I could do about it, and although the result would be catastrophic for me, the likelihood is infinitesimally small. I will choose to just forget about it. I could die in an aircrash, after all, many people have over the years. But I want to keep going on holiday and actually, I really enjoy flying, so again I think I'll forget about that one. And an organisation is no different. As a potential risk owner you could dream up hundreds if not thousands of possible risks which could affect your organisation, but you will need to make a judgement call on which you worry about and which you do not. The key is to establish which risks are out there that would prevent you from achieving your objectives and make that your starting point. This is when you will need to make the conscious decision to not take any action. That is very different don't forget, to not making a decision to do anything.

Linking risks to your objectives sounds fine, and trust me, it works. But how does this work when you are dealing with risks that could have serious impacts on other people? The answer is that you still need to understand how risks link to your own objectives.

Sketch 3

When he isn't avoiding terrorists, Tom works as a transport manager for a travel company, and their main business is transporting customers in their coaches to tourist destinations across Europe. Of course Tom is interested in managing the risks to his customers safety. Proper maintenance of vehicles, making sure that drivers are well trained, qualified and experienced and avoiding natural and manmade hazards in the planning stage are all things he needs to take into account. But the risks will still be clearly linked to his company's objectives.

At a strategic level, Tom's company may have the objective of having a minimum of 80% occupancy on all coach trips (anything less would make the company unsustainable). He needs to consider what risks would stop them achieving that? Loss of customer confidence perhaps, caused by a fatal road accident? So the company is managing customer safety risks whilst managing the risks to their own objectives. This is the nature of strategic risk management. We will see more about how we categorise risk shortly.

Strategic Risk

Strategic risk may sound quite a grand or even pompous title for a small organisation, but the reality is that every organisation exists for a reason and whether or not you call it so or even recognise it, every organisation has a strategy. This being the case every organisation has strategic objectives (the things it wants to achieve) and it follows that there are risks out there which may prevent the organisation from achieving them.

Part of the difficulty many organisations face in trying to determine their strategic risks, is failing to clearly understand or articulate their strategy in the first place.

Again, this is not a book about strategy, there are many eminent authors out there who have produced excellent works on the subject. It does however go without saying that the clearer you are on what your organisation is trying to achieve, then the easier it is to identify the risks that will prevent you from doing it.

So you first have to work out what your organisation wants to achieve at the highest level, and then work out what might happen that would stop you achieving it.

Operational Risk

Operational risks then are the lower level risks that will still cause you problems, but will not in themselves bring your organisation down. There should be a clear line of sight between strategic and operational risks; in other words, you should be conscious of the risks which will stop you achieving the strategy, and then at the next level down, the risks which could contribute to that situation.

In the case above, we could say that in managing the strategic risk of failing to achieve 80% occupancy, we have identified the operational risk that problems with the new online booking system means that it may mistakenly tell people trying to book seats that the coach is full, resulting in less than 80% occupancy.

Articulation of risk

To paraphrase a well known management quote by Charles Kettering, an American inventor and philosopher'

'A risk well stated is a risk half mitigated.'

In my experience an awful lot of the difficulties I have seen people struggling with when trying to manage risks can be traced back to a lack of understanding of what the risk actually is.

We will look firstly at some of the problems or difficulties in articulating risks, and then look at a simple way of ensuring consistency and understanding of what your risks really are.

A risk is made up of three elements:

- Description
- Cause
- Impact or consequence

I will discuss them each individually.

Description

Frequently as discussed briefly in the previous chapter people are talking about risks when in fact they are trying to deal with a problem. Let me say this as clearly as I know how - if there is no uncertainty surrounding an event, in other words if it has happened, is actually happening or will definitely happen sometime in the future, then it isn't a risk it's a problem. There may well be a risk hiding in there somewhere, and you will need to dig a bit deeper to find it. Here however we are dealing with a problem or issue.

Sketch 4

Tom, whom we met earlier, is wrestling with this because he has a problem with his car.

Tom's car is frankly getting on a bit. He has noticed for some time that the brakes are getting softer and softer. The car still stops, but he is worried because his MOT is coming up soon. Tom is talking to a friend and articulates the risk thus:

> *'I have a risk because my car will fail the MOT because the brakes are defective and I won't have any transport to get to work so I'll probably get the sack.'*

This is not a risk; it is a problem and Tom's difficulty starts with how he describes the risk. With defective brakes, the car will fail the MOT. There is no uncertainty surrounding that, it will happen - assuming that Tom takes it to a reputable garage! He is not then dealing with a risk, he is dealing with a problem. The concern here is that Tom doesn't understand the real risk involved, or worse still is simply burying his head in the sand and pretending it isn't there.

In my teaching and training, I always insist that the description of a risk must start by saying 'There is a risk that (something bad might happen)' If you cannot start the description in these terms then the likelihood is that you do not have a risk, you have a problem and you need to go deeper. Sometimes this can seem a little 'Janet and John', but I have had real results with this and have had many people saying that they get it where they previously focussed on problems. Remember, do the basics first.

If Tom uses this approach, his original description will be invalid because there is no uncertainty.

Tom's friend points this out and so he has another attempt.

> *'There is a risk that I will lose my job. This will be caused by my car failing the MOT and I won't be able to drive to work.'*

Here we see another common problem which is jumping straight to the impact. Tom could probably argue that the uncertainty is there in this case. He has other options for getting to work and he has a tolerant boss so it is not certain that he would lose his job. On the face of it then this means the risk articulation works. Examining the real risks that we face can sometimes be uncomfortable and jumping straight to the impact is sometimes an attractive option as it is easier and it can look as if the owner has described the risk properly. This approach misses the point however and all too often the real risks go unnoticed and unmanaged.

Tom's friend recognises the shortcomings in the approach and suggests another attempt. This is the point at which Tom starts to feel very uncomfortable because talking it through the reality of the risk that he is taking starts to hit home. His third attempt is much nearer to the mark.

'There is a risk that I will cause the death or serious injury to another road user in a road traffic accident'.

Cause

This is perhaps the most important part of the articulation, because a lot of what you do to treat the risk will be targeted at the cause. This part of the articulation must start with the words, *'This will be caused by...'*.

This is usually clear and sometimes in fact the risk is raised because a cause has been identified first. Tom knows that his car has defective brakes, what he didn't understand in the first instance was what the risk was that he was facing. Tom's first attempt at describing the cause is,

> *'This will be caused by my car having defective brakes'*

This may be a comfortable way of describing it however it's not particularly helpful. Tom's friend points out that the car has defective brakes right now, but as the car is parked on Tom's driveway is poses no risk to anyone. The very fact that the car has brakes that don't work properly is not the real cause. The uncomfortable truth is that the risk will only be 'caused' if Tom chooses to drive the car in its current condition.

> *'This will be caused by my driving the car with defective brakes'*

It is important to seek out all causes at this point as there may be more than one and different causes may require very different treatments. For example if Tom was partial to a few pints of an evening and regularly drove his car whilst under the influence of alcohol then that could also be a different cause requiring a different treatment.

Impact

This is exactly what it says. If this event were to occur, what would the impact be. It is important to remember that risks need to be aligned to your objectives, so when you are looking at the risks you own, you also need to focus on the impact of a risk on you or your organisation. In the case we are looking at here it would be easy to say that the impact would be that someone would die. That doesn't mean much however to Tom.

He has already said that in the description so to say it here would be just repeating himself.

The purpose of identifying the impact is to allow us to decide if we can do anything to lessen the impact should the risk occur. There may be some treatments Tom could utilise to reduce the impact, but in order to understand what he needs to do to manage the risk, he needs to focus on what the impact would be on him.

The impact of this risk on Tom would be at best a heavy fine and at worst a term in prison. He would lose his job and income, his good name would be lost and probably his health and wellbeing would be damaged as well.

These could be summarised here as

- Financial and penal sanctions
- Reputational damage
- Loss of income
- Ill health

Frequently it is sufficient to summarise the impacts as headings like this, although depending on the circumstances a little more detail may be required. There needs to be sufficient information for the people who have to manage the risk to be able to fully understand it, but not so much that they get bogged down in the details.

Tom has finally got to the point where he can articulate the risk properly.

> *'There is a risk that I will cause the death or serious injury of another road user in a road traffic accident. This will be caused by my driving the vehicle with defective brakes. The impact will be severe financial or penal sanctions, reputational damage loss of income and ill-health brought on by stress and anxiety.*

Key points
- *For anything to be described as a risk, there must be some level of uncertainty*
- *Risks must be linked to objectives*
- *Risk description – 'Something bad might happen'*

Chapter 3

Risk assessment Part 2

Perception

Risk assessment is all about perception. The fact that by its very nature risk involves uncertainty there can be no way of determining the likelihood of something happening or for that matter the impact, with any degree of certainty.

Sure, if you get deep into mathematical modelling of risk and use techniques such as Monte Carlo modelling then you can get closer to certainty but you can never achieve it; if an event was certain it wouldn't be a risk in the first place.

Everyone looks at risk differently. Some people are naturally risk averse, whilst others are happy to take greater risks. Two people may have the same personal goals of happiness and contentment but will seek different risks on the road to achieving them.

A gambler will happily bet the farm on red whilst at the same time travelling everywhere by car because he refuses to fly in an aeroplane which he sees as an inherently risky venture. On the other hand, a thrill seeker who refuses to buy so much as a lottery ticket for fear of losing money will not just fly in an aeroplane, but will strap herself to the top wing of a bi-plane and stand there sporting a big silly grin whilst the pilot throws the aircraft around the sky.

They both face the same risks (losing money or dying in a plane crash), but have polarised perceptions of them. This is an extremely common phenomenon and examples can be seen everywhere. When assessing risks in a business context a risk owner needs to understand that s/he will bring a certain perception to the table of any given risk. This will be informed by life experiences, knowledge, background, position within the organisation, what they have read in the papers, even what they may or may not have had for breakfast.

Everyone else involved however, may have a very different perception and this is where the real fun starts!

If you just left a group of people in a room to talk about a risk and decide what it meant, you would probably be there all day and still come out with widely opposing views at the end of it. For this reason, organisations adopt some form of scoring methodology.

What I am going to talk about for the remainder of this chapter is the method known as the 5x5 scoring system, which is in widespread use not only across the UK, but across the world. The system is not without its limitations, but its simplicity and ease of use allows millions of organisations to have a better understanding of their risk then they would otherwise have had, without spending inordinate amounts of time and money on more detailed assessments.

Likelihood

There really are only two factors that we need to concern ourselves with when assessing a risk; what is the likelihood of it happening, and what will the impact be if it does. First, let us consider likelihood.

Just for clarity, you could just as well use the term probability. Although the terms do have specific technical differences, they are frequently used interchangeably in risk management, to keep things simple we will stick to likelihood.

The 5x5 system requires us to consider the likelihood of an event on a scale of 1 – 5, with 1 being the least likely scenario and 5 being the most likely.

Rather than just say *'Well I think it's a four'* it is customary to put some words to the numbers to give an indication in real terms of what is meant. There are many words that can be used to describe likelihood; probable, possible, unlikely, rarely, frequently are just a few. When I implement a system I advocate using the following terms, which are called descriptors:

- Highly unlikely
- Unlikely
- Likely
- Highly likely
- Almost certain

You can use others of course but the important thing is that you have a sliding scale from the least to the most likely scenario. The reason why I use the terms above in favour of others is that with this scale, there is no middle ground, no safe place to run; risk owners are forced to consider the risk and make a proper decision.

Another version of this scale would be:

- Highly unlikely
- Unlikely
- Possible
- Likely
- Highly likely

The problem with this scale is that it introduces that safe middle ground of 'possible'. The trouble with that is that almost anything is possible. Alright, it is highly unlikely that I would win the X-Factor next year, but here and now it could not be said to be *impossible*. A change in the format of the show, perhaps some different judges (and the small matter of a miraculous improvement in my singing) could certainly not rule it out so you could therefore argue that it is possible.

The problem I am trying to highlight, is that when you put this safe middle ground, people can tend to gravitate to it because it is safe and frankly easier. The centre of my preferred scale is skewed (when looking at the numbers it falls between 2 and 3) which forces people to think more carefully about the score they assign.

In addition to the descript*or*, I always add a descript*ion*, which is intended to help people further when deciding which descriptor to use.

For example, to describe almost certain, I will say something like *'Significant historical and/or other evidence exists to suggest that this risk will almost certainly occur'*.

Finally, certainly when dealing with operational risk, I always ask people to consider what is the likelihood of the risk occurring *within the next 5 years*. The reason for this is twofold. Firstly 5 years is a typical planning window for organisations and secondly if you look at the likelihood of something *ever* happening, then most things would fall into the almost certain bracket (me winning the X-Factor excepted).

If you tell people to focus on the next 5 years the chances are that you will get a more realistic assessment of a risk.

Impact

Again we need to use a scale of 1 – 5 and assign descriptors and descriptions to each one and again there are many words that you can use to describe impacts; I tend to use the following five terms. These terms are called descriptors.

- Insignificant
- Minor
- Moderate
- Major
- Critical

It is not quite so easy to avoid that safe middle ground here, but over the years I have found that these terms work best in most organisations. You will occasionally see the last one, '*Critical*', replaced by the word '*Catastrophic*'.

Whilst there is nothing inherently wrong with this word in this context, it is a very emotive term which generally conjures up images of death and destruction, with volcanoes erupting, aircraft falling out of the sky, meteors crashing into cities, nuclear fall-out... sorry, getting a bit carried away there, but you get the point. I have found that the term people can be reluctant to use the term catastrophic and are much happier with the term critical. At the end of the day it is only a word, and if realising a risk could mean the complete failure of your organisation then that could indeed be described as catastrophic. At the end of the day, the culture of your own organisation will determine which of these is more acceptable.

But these are just simple words. We will see shortly how we can put some context into them.

Risk Proximity

Risk proximity is a term I have come across many times in project risk management, particularly in Prince 2™ methodology. In this methodology a project is divided up into Stages, which run consecutively. When you are managing a project with 5 or six discreet stages, you may well have risks which are going to be identified at the outset, but will not actually manifest until a later stage, weeks or possibly even months after the project is initiated. Proximity allows the project manager to categorise risks with terms like 'Imminent', 'Next Stage' or even 'On project completion'.

A project using this methodology should not proceed from one stage to another without proper sign off and authorisation. In this case considering proximity can be a useful way of prioritising resources. There is little point in spending valuable resource in mitigating a risk that cannot happen yet, and may never happen if the project doesn't get that far. For this reason, it can sometimes be helpful to refer to the proximity of a risk.

I have seen and heard example however of where people are trying to get this to fit into everyday risk management, but in my opinion it simply doesn't work. If you identify a risk to your objectives, then the risk exists and should be managed. Adding in proximity in this system can confuse matters, and can make the scoring very complicated. Again, you will need to check your own system, but considering proximity for business risk is not something I would recommend.

Risk Categorisation

Describing the impacts of a risk is all about dividing your risks into categories, sometimes called domains. This means starting to think about what risks you are really concerned about and which ones not quite so much. As risk owners, most of you will have these decisions already made for you by your risk managers. Those of you setting up your own systems in a small business for instance will need to do this for yourselves.

The question then, is what type of risks are you going to get excited about?

Let's start with a common risk that most organisations will be concerned with and that is financial risk.

To help you as a risk owner to decide on the correct impact level, the organisation needs to describe them in the same way that we described likelihood earlier. This starts with the descriptors that we just saw, but then for each descriptor there will be a description.

These descriptions will be very specific to the organisation. For example, a large multi-national pharmaceutical manufacturer is unlikely to get too worried about an impact of £50,000, but it could be catastrophic to a small business.

Again for most of you risk owners this will already have been done for you, but some of you will need to at least participate in the exercise to identify the impact descriptions. Most organisations will develop an impact table which will list the risk categories which they are concerned about on one axis, and the 5 levels on the other. Each level for each category will then have a corresponding description.

The coach company we saw earlier then may have a list of risk categories that looks like this:

- Passenger Safety
- Financial
- Reputational
- Staff welfare
- Business Continuity
- Environmental

It depends entirely on what matters to the company. In this case they are clearly going to be concerned about passenger safety, but obviously would have no interest in say clinical risk. It is now that the descriptions will be required. So for example the coach company may say that for passenger safety the term Insignificant might be described as:

No passenger injury, possible minor distress caused.

At the other end a Critical impact could be described as:

Death or life changing injury to one or more passengers.

The intervening descriptions would then be gradually increasing in terms of severity.

How an organisation categorises risk is important, because it makes it possible to make assessments on the possible impacts of risks if they occur and also helps greatly in setting the organisation's risk appetite. As this book is about risk ownership however and not risk management in a wide context, I will leave the reader to consult their own policy and system to see what categories and descriptions of risk your organisation wants you to be concerned about.

It is important to keep in mind however that these are only descriptions of what any given risk might look like. They should never be interpreted too literally. For example your risk descriptions may mean that a financial impact of *'Up to £500,000'* would mean a major risk, whilst an impact of *'In excess of £500,000'* would mean that the same risk was described as critical. Now it is surely clear that when dealing with a loss of around half a million pounds, we are not going to act dramatically differently if the loss is expected to be

£499,999 then we will if it is £500,001; it's a pretty big loss regardless of the odd couple of quid difference.

You should regard descriptions as a guide only to your decision making, and don't try and interpret them too mathematically or literally. Remember risk management isn't an exact science, so don't try and make it so.

Severity

Having decided what the likelihood and what the impact is of any given risk, we now need to determine the severity. This is done by taking the two scores and multiplying them together whilst at the same time plotting them on a risk matrix.

The point of a risk matrix (also known as a risk map or heat map), is to present a visual depiction of where a risk sits in relation to the organisations risk appetite and tolerance levels.

The risk map can also give an impression of an organisation's overall risk appetite.

Risk maps are typically colour coded with the colours that the organisation chooses to use to rate the severity of their risks. A great many organisations use a simple traffic light system of red, amber and green (also known as RAG) to rate their risks as high, moderate or low. Some however will introduce a fourth colour (usually utilising different shades of yellow or amber) and adding a fourth severity category such as extreme. As the risk maps used are shown in black and white (if you are reading the Kindle version), I use the following key to distinguish between the colours. To see the risk maps in all their colourful glory, please head on over to my website at www.metisrisk.co.uk/professionalriskowner

Shading	Colour	Description
	Green	Low Risk
	Amber	Moderate Risk
	Red	High Risk

For our purposes we are going to assume that your organisation uses a standard risk map as shown in the figure below. (Note that in these examples the risk descriptors have been left out in favour of the score simply for clarity's sake)

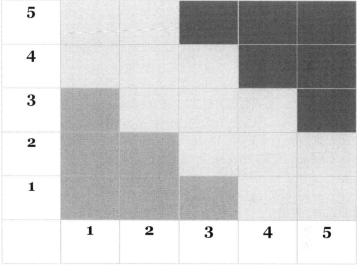

Fig 1. Symmetrical risk map (risk neutral)

This type of risk map can be said to be symmetrical for reasons which I trust would be clear. An organisation using this type of map can be said to be risk neutral. The red and the green areas on the map are equal in area. Assuming then that sufficient risks of varying severity are plotted, this suggests that there is likely to be a fair spread of risks across the map, and there is no greater likelihood of a risk being scored high or low (as opposed to moderate).

Consider the following example though of an asymmetric risk map.

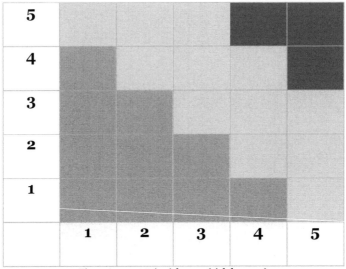

Fig 2. Asymmetric risk map (risk hungry)

Would you say that an organisation using this map would be more or less keen on taking risk?

Assuming the same spread of risks as previously, in this case the spread is more likely to end up skewed towards the green or amber than the red simply because the red area is so small. This would suggest that the organisation is more keen to take risks that if they were using the risk neutral map in Fig 1. The organisation could be said to be risk hungry.

Finally, if the risk map were asymmetric but in the opposite direction, then it would suggest that the organisation is less keen to take risks as more of their risks are likely to appear as high. Any company using a risk map such as this could be said to be risk averse.

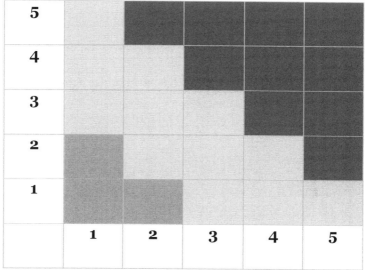

Fig 3. Asymmetric risk map (risk averse)

I am of course making generalisations here and other factors would need to be taken into account. I am also making the assumption that the organisation is using the particular risk map with at least some level of knowledge of why and how it works, but looking at your organisation's risk map can give you a good indicator as to what their attitude to risk might be.

Reasonable worst case scenario

Sometimes when assessing and scoring risks there could be a range of different impacts and likelihoods. Perhaps there might be a very low likelihood of the risk occurring with a major impact, but an almost certainty existing that it will occur with a very minor one. This is where the subjectivity becomes even more apparent and in cases like this, it is necessary to assess the risk against the 'reasonable worst case scenario'. This goes back to what I said in Chapter 2 that many more things can happen that actually will. What the risk owner needs to do now is to consider all the possibilities and then think for each risk what in their mind is this reasonable worst case scenario, the key word here being reasonable.

Sketch 5

The company that Tom works for is located 200 yards from the end of the runway at a busy commercial airport and directly under the flight path. His boss is always on about their 'Business Continuity' plan and wanting to be sure that Tom is up to speed on it. Just in case she says there should be an aircraft accident nearby meaning they couldn't get into their premises. Tom knows quite a bit about aeroplanes and queries why the other premises that the company owns does not require the same level of planning. They are, he argues under a major crossroads in the sky with literally hundreds of aircraft passing overhead every day and so the risks surely apply there as well. But Tom's boss explains that where they are, an aircraft accident is a reasonable worst case scenario, whereas the other location whilst obviously technically possible the same level of planning would not be proportionate, as the likelihood is considerably lower. She also explains to Tom that he watches the Discovery Channel far too often!

Only you and your organisation can decide what is reasonable.

If your decisions were ever to be questioned, then the well-established test of reasonableness will come down to what your average person without specialist knowledge of the subject would consider to be a reasonable decision on the issue.

One of the best known legal tests of this is the oft-quoted 'man on the Clapham omnibus'. A full discussion on this is beyond the scope of this book, but if you place the term into your chosen search engine I am quite sure you will find plenty of quality bed-time reading.

Inherent risk score

When you have calculated the severity here, you have calculated the first of three 'scores' with which we need to concern ourselves – the Inherent Risk score.

Sometimes called the Raw risk score, inherent risk is the severity score attracted by the risk, before you take any account of the controls you have in place already to manage it. Now this is where I will deviate from some of my colleagues in certain disciplines in risk management, notably Health and Safety, where the inherent risk frequently takes account of existing controls at the time of the assessment. We will come onto that in a minute but for now take my word for it that as a risk owner, you need this 'raw' score.

The score here will often be quite high, but when you calculate the next score you will probably see that fall. But before we come on to the second score, let's talk a little about risk control.

Key points
- *Risk is a matter of perception*
- *Many more things can happen than will – remember the reasonable worst case scenario*
- *The inherent risk score is vitally important to understand what steps need to be taken to manage risks*

Chapter 4

Fortune telling

Of course, a key thing to always bear in mind here is that you don't have any certainty. The best you can do is to make a prediction of what the likelihood and the impact might look like; an estimate if you will. And how good are you at this? It turns out not quite as good as you probably think you are.

If I asked you to predict the likelihood that you would be late for work in the next month what would you say? If I were asked I would think about my past performance and most likely say that I haven't been late in the last two years therefore it is highly unlikely that I will be late in the next month. Does that sound reasonable to you?

You make predictions like this all the time. Perhaps unconsciously you made that particular prediction when you applied for the job, after all who takes a job knowing that the chances of turning up on time every day are slim? Yet how many times have you been stuck in traffic in the morning? How many times has your train been running late (I'm told that they do once in a while), or have the kids been playing up over breakfast? And how many times have you actually had a near miss, running through the door with 2 minutes to go? Does your prediction take account of this? Perhaps it does, but if you are like most of us mere mortals it probably doesn't. Nicholas Nasim Taleb in his book, The Black Swan calls this 'The illusion of understanding' and he goes on to describe how we think we know what's going on in the world, but in reality we frequently don't.

But not only are we poor predictors of the future, we're not particularly good at estimating things either. You make estimates every day, and they are estimates because you do not and indeed cannot know the full picture; it has not yet happened. The trouble is that because we do it all the time and mostly get it right, we get lulled into a false sense of security. You find it easy to make estimates about everyday things because you do it...well, every day. You estimate how long your journey to work will be, when your coffee is cool enough to drink, and whether you can get to your destination without needing a comfort break (one of my favourite euphemisms) because you have lots of experience of this stuff.

Aside from the trivialities of everyday life, professionals are involved in estimating as a matter of routine. The builder will estimate how many bricks he will need to buy in order to build your extension, without knowing for certain how many breakages there will be, or how many he may need to reject. The estate agent will estimate how much your house will sell for, without knowing the circumstances of the people who are likely to buy, and how much they are prepared to pay. And the mechanic will estimate how much your car will cost to repair, without knowing for certain the condition of the unseen parts which may need to be replaced.

We all draw on what we know and our estimates draw on a variety of sources of information. In the same way as I described how risk itself is a matter of perception and we are all informed by our experiences and knowledge, the same can be said of estimating. So what happens when you get it wrong? Let's not sugar coat this; you will from time to time get it wrong, there really is no way of getting away from it.

Estimating the impact of an event is slightly easier than the likelihood in my experience, because you can describe what the impact would look like. I know that if my car gets stolen, the financial impact is going to be the value of the car plus any additional expenses that I would incur in travelling. I wouldn't know exactly how much it would still be an estimate, but I can be fairly confident that I won't be a long way off. If I were to try and estimate the likelihood however that is a very different. The insurance company makes this estimate when they decide how much to charge me, and then

I make the estimate every time I park it somewhere. Again, we are both pretty good at it (I haven't had a car stolen in 30 years), so both myself and the insurance company could estimate the likelihood of it happening being highly unlikely.

It is important to recognise however that just because you assess the likelihood as being highly unlikely, doesn't mean it won't happen today. I have been in emergency planning and business continuity management in one form or another for around 15 years, and I have lost count of the number of 1 in 400 year events or 1 in 1000 year events that I have seen. So if you assess an event as highly unlikely and it happens the following day, does this make your original estimate invalid? No of course not.

Go back for a moment to my earlier question about the likelihood of you being late for work. Let's say for arguments sake the estimate is highly unlikely. This doesn't mean that it cannot happen tomorrow, and also the next day and the next day. But then it may not happen again for another seven years. Three times in seven years sounds highly unlikely to me, so does that validate the original estimate? There is no right or wrong answer to this, so I will leave you to make your own judgement.

The fundamental problem with estimating is that because we do it so often, frequently sub-consciously, and we are pretty good at it, we become over confident in our ability to produce accurate estimates. I'm sorry to say that there really is no silver bullet here, this is the loneliness of the risk owner's chair. You will have to make decisions with various amounts of information of variable quality, all the time not knowing what the future holds, and you are likely to think that your estimates are more accurate than they really are. Douglas Hubbard who I mentioned earlier in his other excellent work, 'How To Measure Anything – finding the value of intangibles in business', has done much work on this issue and describes how we can be trained and 'calibrated' to make more accurate estimates. For the majority of us however, we will just have to keep doing the best that we can, whilst understanding our limitations. Further discussion on this is beyond the scope of this book, but I would highly recommend Hubbard's work to anyone who is interested in the field of decision making in risk management.

Key points
- *Nobody knows the future, you can but predict*
- *Beware the confident estimate – they can be wildly inaccurate*
- *Just because something is highly unlikely, doesn't mean it won't happen tomorrow*

Chapter 5

Risk Controls

Bearing in mind as we said earlier that a risk involves the likelihood of something bad happening, a control is something designed or intended to reduce the likelihood of the risk happening, or to reduce the impact if it does. Controls are sometimes called mitigations.

But before we can even consider something to be a control, it must have 3 essential elements.

1. It must exist.

This will sound obvious and even flippant but trust me it isn't. It is extremely common to have controls listed against risks which contain words like planned, intended or anticipated. But if you are talking about something in the future tense, then more than likely you do not have a control. You may have one at some point in the future, but you are concerned with now, not tomorrow. You can have all the aspirations in the world, but if something doesn't actually exist today, it is not controlling the risk today. It really is as simple as that.

2. It must act upon the risk it is supposed to control

That means this risk, at this time. Not some other risk, or some problem, it must be acting upon this specific risk.

3. It must be something that you control

That means exactly what it says, you are in control of it or at least your organisation is. Something which is in the control of a third party is very difficult to manage with any certainty. It may be acting upon the risk, but if it is beyond your control it is difficult to assess how effective it is, and obvious though it sounds, you cannot control it. For you to be comfortable with your risk management, you need to understand how much control you have over them and blindly accepting controls which you cannot yourself control will provide you with nothing more than a false sense of security.

Having got your control to the starting gate we now need to describe it effectively. In some cases, particularly where we talk about health and safety risks, controls can be quite obvious. Guardrails, Personal Protective Equipment (PPE), warning signs and physical security locks that prevent entry to unauthorised persons are all good examples of controls. But how do we control business risks?

It is necessary here to think beyond the obvious. You will almost always have a gut feeling that the inherent risk score is too high because you are doing something to reduce it. You just have to be able to identify and articulate what it is that you are doing. You might have regular discussions at your management team meetings – that could be a control. Or you might have a contingency plan or a documented set of Standard Operating Procedures. You have an agreed budget to deal with something, or an IT solution that reduces your risk exposure. Any of these things can be classed as controls, as long as they meet the requirements set out above i.e. they exist, they act upon that risk and they are within your control.

This issue of who controls the control is particularly important. Tom again can help with this point:

Sketch 5
Tom has aspirations to buy his own home, but he is acutely aware that there is a risk that he may not be able to afford to buy a house in line with his plans. This will be caused amongst other things by an unaffordable interest rate rise and the impact will be that he will fail to meet his strategic goal (owning his own home).

Now Tom may be able to put some mitigations in to control this risk. He may for example increase his savings every month, or limit his outgoings by not taking on loans or HP agreements. There is a limit however to how much he personally can control this risk.

The Bank of England exercises tight control over interest rates and so they are certainly controlling the risk, but as an individual, Tom probably doesn't sit too highly on their list of priorities. That coupled with the unfortunate fact that Tom doesn't sit on the bank's Monetary Policy Committee means Tom is not in a position to 'control' this control. So, whilst he may have his other controls in place he cannot rely on the controls that are the sole responsibility of the Bank of England – the status of that particular control could change at any time.

This is the inherent problem with controls which are solely the responsibility of a third party. They can change, weaken, fail or simply disappear and you might not even know until it is too late.

It is essential however that you know whether or not the controls that you do have are effective and for this reason each control must have at least one assurance to go with it. We will discuss assurances in Chapter 5.

Another thing you need to understand about controls is the relationship between controls and resources.

For the sake of argument, you have a risk with a likelihood score of five (Almost Certain). You are completely unhappy with this and want to reduce the likelihood to one (Highly Unlikely). The cost of the controls required (in resources – not just money), to reduce the risk down from five to four would be £X. How much would it cost to bring it down to three. Probably twice as much you say. Unlikely I say. In real terms it is more likely to be £X^2. So what about reducing it to two then, £X3? Probably. The cost of implementing controls increases exponentially in most cases, in other words the more you try and control a risk the more it is going to cost you. And don't forget you cannot manage a risk down to impossible. You will only continue to make it less and less likely to occur (or less and less of an impact). If it is truly impossible then it doesn't exist which means you have managed to terminate the activity.

What this also means is that the effect of the controls is usually inversely proportionate to the cost. In other words, early controls that are relatively cheap in terms of resource can have quite an effect on the risk; after all if you were doing nothing and now you are doing something that must have an effect right? But the more you try to control the risk, and the more resource you throw at it, gradually the effect on the risk you are managing decreases until at the end you could be throwing huge amounts of cash at a risk to have only a minimal further effect on it.

This is where the value of a cost benefit analysis comes in, because there is little point in spending £20,000 to reduce a financial risk that at worst could cost you £10,000 even if it happened (which is far from certain.)

Control owners

In the same way that all risks need an owner, all controls must have an owner. The role of the control owner is to manage the control and to provide assurances to the risk owner that the control is effective.

All sorts of people can be control owners, it depends entirely on what the control is, and in many ways it is similar to risk ownership. The owner must have some level of responsibility and decision making power for the control in question.

Again in small businesses, it may well be the case that the risk owner is also the control owner. Whatever the case, the risk owner will need to be satisfied that the control is effective and is doing what it is supposed to.

Key points
- **Three elements controls must have:**
    - ○ **Exist**
    - ○ **Act upon the risk**
    - ○ **Be within your control**
- **All controls must have an owner**
- **All controls must have at least one assurance**

Chapter 6

Risk assessment Part 3

Okay, so now we know what controls are, we need to start looking at what the actual risk is today. This assessment is called the residual risk score.

Like most things I am describing to you, this is quite a subjective assessment. You need to check first that your assessment score from part 1 is correct – the inherent risk score. Once you are satisfied that it's right, check out the controls that you have in place and decide how effective they are. Don't forget as we discussed earlier, the controls must satisfy three conditions before they can even be considered, i.e. they must exist, they must act upon the risk and they must be within your control.

Once you are satisfied that the controls meet these criteria, then you will need to consult your control owners and determine how effective they are. This is probably a good time to consider an important distinction in risk management; the one between assurance and re-assurance.

Assurance v. Re-assurance

Sketch 6

Tom is trying to persuade his girlfriend to go out on the town on Saturday evening and he knows that she is more likely to say yes if he says they will stay in a local hotel and make a proper night out of it. Tom has two options then:
He can say *'Yes that's great, and when we have had enough we'll just go around to the pub we usually stay at and I'm sure they will have a room available, after all we have never been turned away before.'*

Or the other option he has, is he can email the hotel in advance and pay them a deposit to reserve their room, to which he will get a (hopefully) positive response, again by email.

With option 1, he can provide his girlfriend with a degree of *re-assurance*. He knows where they will go, they have stayed there before so they know that they like it, and they have always managed to get a room when they have wanted one. Tom can give quite a lot of re-assurance and depending on what mood she is in and how badly she wants a night out, she may accept that because it will make her feel OK. If his girlfriend were to be completely honest however, she would still have a slight nagging feeling in the back of her mind. What if they don't have any rooms, what if they are closed for refurbishment, what if they are full because they have a wedding going on?

What Tom is not providing her with at this point, is any *assurance*.

With option 2 he can tell her that the pub has confirmed the room, and he can even show her the email confirmation and the receipt for payment. So now they can go out and enjoy the evening safe in the knowledge that they have done all that they can to secure a bed for the night and they aren't going to be sleeping on the beach.

Tom can never be 100% certain that something won't go horribly wrong. They could have made a mistake and double booked, or the pub could get blown apart in a gas explosion! But in reality he has done all that he reasonably can, and they can both take reasonable assurance from that. This is exactly how risk assurances work.

As the risk owner you should be seeking assurance from your control owners, not simply re-assurance. In the same way if you have people to answer to they will be seeking the same.

The distinction between the two can sometimes be subtle, but assurance is usually characterised by something tangible; something you can see or read. Re-assurance on the other hand is putting your arm around someone's shoulder and telling them *'everything will be fine'*. Accepting re-assurance is effectively taking someone's word for it that things are OK. Now if it's simply a night out at stake, then an arm around the shoulder may be fine, but what if it's more than that. If you are talking to one of your control owners about their controls, what would you prefer, assurance or re-assurance?

Assurance can take many forms and it will depend very much on your organisation, but some links between controls and assurances to get you started in your thinking are shown in the table below.

Control	Assurances
Fire Extinguisher	Maintenance record
Management meeting	Minutes
	Output reports
	Terms of Reference
Standard Operating Procedures	Training Records
	Incident reports
	Accident reports
Contingency plans	Training records
	Exercise reports
	Incident reports

Fig 4 Controls and associated assurances

Only you can decide as the risk owner how much assurance you need but the greater the risk, the more robust your assurance will probably need to be.

So you seek the assurances you need to and then you have to decide how much of an effect the controls are having on your risk. You need to satisfy yourself that the controls are effective or not as the case may be.

Like so many other elements of risk management, this is very much a subjective exercise, but it pays to be brutally honest. As the risk owner you need to have a clear understanding of how much control you have over a risk.

Residual risk score

Once you have identified all the controls that are acting upon the risk, then you can re-score it. This is the same process as you went through earlier, and this will then give you the second score that you will need, the residual risk score.

This is sometimes referred to as the 'current risk score'. I have never liked this term as it can be quite misleading. It is the score at the time that the assessment was made, not the time at which you are looking at it. This will become clearer when we look at risk registers a little later on.

For a moment though, let's consider the relationship between the inherent and the residual risk scores because this is where the importance of understanding the difference becomes clear.

The area between the inherent and the residual risk scores is known as the 'control environment'.

Let's say for example that your inherent score is 5/5, that is both the likelihood and the impact come out as 5 so your severity score is 25. That's as high as it can get on our risk map. This means that if you do not do anything about it, the risk is almost certainly going to occur, with a critical impact upon your business.

Once you have looked at the controls though, you re-score it as 5/4, with a residual score of 20. So you have very little difference between the inherent and residual scores. What does this tell you about your control environment? Well it could tell you a number of things:

- That you have very few controls in place
- That your controls are not very effective
- That one or more of your risk scores are wrong

But what it is most likely telling you, is that the controls you have in place are simply not doing very much to control the risk. In this case they are having very little effect on the impact and not reducing the likelihood at all.

Now that isn't necessarily a bad thing. In some cases, it may be that this is just the way it is. By the nature of the risk, you are doing all that can be done and the risk score is still that high. We will see in a moment how we decide if we are happy or not, but for the moment let's have another look at the control environment.

Let's say that instead of the residual risk score coming out at 5/4 it actually comes out at 1/5. This means that you have an inherent score of 25 and a residual score of 5, in other words you have a large difference between the two scores. What does this now tell you about the control environment? Again it could tell you a number of things, pretty much the opposite of what you had earlier:

- That you have a lot of controls in place
- That your controls are very effective
- That your scores are wrong

But it is probably telling you (assuming that your assurances are satisfactory) that the controls are doing a lot to control the risk.

It is however also telling you something else, something equally if not more important. If you have a large difference between the inherent risk score and the residual risk score, you have a great deal of dependence on the controls. Assuming that everything is correct and you haven't mis-scored anything, then you are very reliant on those controls to do their job and if those controls fail you could be in some degree of trouble.

In this case that you need to be very certain that those controls are effective, which brings us back around the loop to examining the controls.

Now that we have determined what our level of exposure is to the risk in question, we come to the first big question. Are we happy with this, or are we going to do something about it?

Key points

- *Assurance and re-assurance are not the same thing*
- *The residual risk score is determined when you take into account the controls in place*
- *The gap between the inherent and residual risk scores tells you how dependant you are on the control environment – the greater the gap the greater the dependency*

Chapter 7

Risk decision making, appetite and tolerance

There are whole books dedicated to the art and science of decision making and it is not my intention to delve into the topic in that level of detail. However, there are some key issues around decision making in risk management that need to be considered.

Having identified and then assessed the risk, this is the point where you can confirm that you are the owner (or not as the case may be). This is a simple test.

There are only four decisions you can make in relation to the management of any given risk; this is commonly referred to as the '4T approach'.

- You can Terminate the risk
- You can Transfer the risk
- You can Treat the risk
- You can Tolerate the risk

If you are to own a risk, you must be able to make one of those four decisions. If you do not have the authority to make those decisions, then you cannot own that risk.

Think back for a moment to Tom's car problem and let's consider what options he has when it comes to decision making on the risk around his car's brakes.

Terminate the risk

What this effectively means is that instead of accepting the risk, Tom will terminate the activity which leads to it. This could happen in a number of ways:

- Tom could stop driving the car and choose to walk or use public transport instead.
- He could have the brakes repaired,
- He could sell the car (declaring the defective brakes obviously!) and buy a new one.

Any one of these would not merely reduce the risk, but eliminate or terminate it, although it could be argued that repairing the brakes would only reduce the risk and not completely eliminate it.

Transfer the risk

This again is an area subject to much confusion and misunderstanding. The most commonly used form of risk transference is insurance, where one person pays another an amount of money (a premium) to get the other person to take on the risk for them. In Tom's case, he will have insured his car to cover the financial aspects of the risk (let's not confuse the issue here with the question of whether or not the insurance would pay out as the car is defective) and so he has transferred some of his risk to the insurance company.

Organisationally you can transfer risk by buying insurance and some risks can be transferred by outsourcing activities. A very important consideration however, and there really is no way of getting around this, is that no matter what you do you cannot transfer your reputational risks. Your reputation will always be yours and no transferring or outsourcing arrangements can ever change that regardless of how much you pay. Reputation truly is priceless.

A common misunderstanding of risk transference however is thinking that you can transfer a risk within your own organisation because you don't have the resource to carry out required actions. This is not transferring a risk.

Treat the risk

In this case the obvious treatment is to get the brakes fixed. As we have seen however that doesn't merely treat the risk it terminates it. If we are going to treat it (which implies that Tom is going to continue to drive the car with defective brakes) then he needs to come up with something different. Some treatment options which Tom could consider are:

- Deciding not to carry passengers. This would reduce the likelihood of the risk because now it could only be someone outside of the car who go killed and not inside (Remember what we said about decisions being palatable?)

- Deciding to drive at a reduced speed and not exceed say 20mph anywhere. This would give him more time to react and stop and therefore reduce the likelihood.

- Deciding to use the roads at quieter times or even quieter roads so that there are fewer people about, again reducing the likelihood.

There may well be moral, legal and even practical questions about any of these treatments, but nevertheless they would all do something to reduce the risk. These are all decisions within the gift of the risk owner, regardless of how palatable they may or may not be.

Tolerate the risk

If this is Tom's decision, then his intention is to continue to drive the car in its current condition, changing none of his behaviour; in other words, nothing changes. He is prepared to put up with this risk exactly as it is, and so no action plan is required.

There are a couple of caveats to the principle that you cannot own risks where you cannot make decision. Firstly, the decision to transfer will not always be available, in fact it will rarely be available; there are some risks that you simply cannot just transfer for example reputation as we have just discussed. It may also be the case that you are not empowered to decide to terminate one of your organisations activities, but provided you have the decision making authority around treating or tolerating you can still be the owner. This situation will not occur too frequently if the risks are correctly articulated.

Finally, there will be occasions where you can own a risk, you will want to treat it but don't have the budget or the resources to do so, and then you have a different option known as escalation. We will cover that in a following chapter. This is where it really becomes key to make absolutely sure that the ownership is at the right level. The fewer your freedom to make decision, the less appropriate it is for you to be the owner of the risk.

Risk appetite and tolerance

Your risk decisions should be driven by your risk appetite and tolerance levels.

This is another one of those concepts in risk management which is consistently misunderstood and misapplied. Depending on where you look you will find many different interpretations of these terms. Some organisations use the terms interchangeably and some choose one or the other and stick to it throughout their system.

ISO31000 which is the International Standard for Risk Management makes no reference to the term risk appetite and so organisations following or aligning to this standard are left to their own devices to come up with a definition should they choose to. The dictionary definition reads:

'A natural desire to satisfy a bodily need, especially for food' or 'A strong desire or liking for something'[2]

This suggests that one actively wants to pursue something and this indeed is the way that you should approach the concept of risk appetite. To understand what our risk appetite is, we need to ask the question,
'How much risk are we willing to accept in pursuit of our objectives'.

Appetite

Risk appetite then is about actively considering the risks that you face and then making a decision about which ones you are prepared to accept and at what level. Managing business risk is a business decision. A business may identify a high risk in terms of its reputation say, or its financial wellbeing. Generally the business is free to make decisions about how well it manages the risk and how much it is prepared to invest to do so.

Risk appetite needs to be set at the highest level of the organisation, usually the Board. The Board will determine its appetite for risk in pursuit of its strategic objectives and these must be communicated throughout the organisation so that managers at all levels understand what risks they are empowered to take and what control measures they must deploy.

Tolerance

---

[2] Oxford Dictionary On-line 2017

Tolerance and appetite are different things. If appetite is the amount of risk you are willing to accept in pursuit of your objectives, tolerance is the amount of risk you are prepared to put up with. In an ideal world, you might like it to be lower but that is not always possible or even desirable. Tolerance may be a temporary state, or could be your final position on a risk and there will be times when your appetite and tolerance for any given risk are at the same level.

For example, when assessing a risk you determine it as being high but your appetite for the risk in question is only moderate. You therefore want to manage the risk down. You tolerate the higher risk until you manage it down to an acceptable level. Once you have reached that level however you continue to tolerate it as you don't intent taking any further action.

At this point your appetite and tolerance are at the same level. However, a change in circumstances may mean that your appetite could move up or down which would call for action to adjust your tolerance level.

It is important to maintain this distinction between appetite and tolerance even when they might appear mathematically the same. Understanding what risk you are actively pursuing and what you are prepared to put up with is crucial to effective risk management.

Next steps

So these are the steps you have taken so far. You have identified and assessed the risk, you have considered the controls and decided how effective they are, you have re-scored the risk, you have determined that you are the owner and taking into account your appetite and tolerance levels you have made a decision. What's next?

Key points

- *There are only four decisions you can take with risks:*
  - *Terminate*
  - *Transfer*
  - *Treat*
  - *Tolerate*
- *Just because the only available decisions may be ones that you don't like, doesn't mean that you don't own the risk. The key point is whether or not you have the power to make them.*
- *Risk appetite is what you want to actively pursue – risk tolerance is what you will put up with*
- *You can NEVER transfer your reputational risks*

Chapter 8

Risk Action Planning

Having made the decision, do you now need an action plan? Well that depends on what decision you have made.

If you have decided to tolerate the risk, then strictly speaking there should be no need for an action plan. If you have already decided that you are happy to accept the risk at the level it is and with the controls in place that you have, why would you need an action plan? In all probability you are right. If however you are thinking that you will tolerate but still have things you want to do about it, I would ask yourself a question. Are you really happy with the level of risk and is tolerate the right decision? It may be that the risk is concerning you more than you first think.

If however you have decided to treat, terminate or transfer the risk, then these things are not going to happen on their own, and the only way to have any assurance (as opposed to re-assurance) that they are going to be effectively managed is to develop an action plan.

Target Risk Score

Having considered all these things and decided that you are not prepared to tolerate the risk, you now need to decide how much you want to treat it. This brings you to the final of the three scores, the target risk score.

Same process as previously, you just need to decide now what likelihood and impact levels you will be happy with. Once you have set your targets, look at the difference between the residual and target scores. Remember how the bigger the difference between inherent and residual scores, the more reliant you are on the controls? Well here, the bigger the difference between the residual and target scores, the more action planning you will need to do.

The one key issue here however is that if your decision has been to either treat, transfer or terminate a risk, then your target score must be less than your residual score. Obviously, there are few scenarios where you would want your target to be greater than the residual anyway, but the point I am making is that it can't be the same, it must be less. If the decision is to tolerate, then the target score will probably be the same although it isn't necessarily the case.

Action Planning

When it comes to action planning, there is no rocket science attached to this, action planning is action planning in my book whether it be for a project, a risk or planning your own holiday. You simply decide where you need to be and work out how you are going to get there.

Call me old fashioned, but I like SMART action planning, if done properly you really can't go wrong.

I don't intend going into a full description of SMART planning in this book but a quick refresh would probably not go amiss.

S – Specific

Make your action very clear and specific. If it is, then it is easy to tell when you have achieved it. A specific action would be 'I will develop a standard operating procedure (SOP) for x'. You will immediately know when you have achieved that – you will have the approved document in front of you. If your action says however 'I will continue to review and monitor SOPs', that really doesn't tell you much and will be tricky to see when you have achieved it.

M – Measureable

This very much follows on, make sure that you will be able to tell when the action is completed. The two examples above illustrate this point, the first is clearly measureable, the second is not.

A – Achievable

Is your action a realistic target? I can set an action in my personal development plan that I will complete my PhD project by the end of this year. Given that I have only just started this is completely unrealistic and almost certainly not achievable.

That should not stop you setting challenging targets however, but you do need to have a sense of realism attached to them as well.

R – Relevant

This one is perhaps the most important. The action needs to be relevant to the risk that you are trying to control. This means that every action should have some degree of impact on your control environment and should be bringing the residual risk score a step closer to the target score. It should be doing something to control the risk, or at least be working towards it.

You will not necessarily find that each action will result in a new control in themselves, but they should in total be adding sufficient additional controls to get your score down to your target. If your actions are not going to bring the score down to the target, then you're simply not trying hard enough. Your action plan appears incomplete.

Only you will know, when you consider your organisation whether or not the actions will achieve this.

T – Timebound

Make sure with your actions that you set a clear target date for when they will need to be completed. This again will depend very much on your risk appetite and tolerance levels.

Action Owners

Don't forget that each action will require an owner – someone who is accountable for delivery. This may be you, but frequently it will not. For example you may have a business problem that requires an IT solution. Unless you are also the Head of the IT department you probably cannot complete the actions required here, but will have to assign that action to someone who can.

This is where things can start to get tricky and it's very easy here to find that things are 'falling through the cracks'.

There needs to be a very clear assignment of action here, and that includes an acceptance by the action owner that they have the action and will deliver it on time. In a small organisation that may well be a simple case of talking to your colleague and making it happen.

In larger organisations however, particularly where different departments have very clear objectives themselves, they may not feel the need to prioritise your risk and the action can get delayed or even ignored. As the risk owner, you will need to be satisfied that the actions required to mitigate or control your risk effectively are being given the attention the deserve. In short you need some assurance that it will get done.

This is where you need to have another option, when the action to deal with a risk is simply not within your gift.

You have decided that you own a risk, you are not prepared to tolerate it, but it is not within your gift to do anything about it. The best option now, is to escalate it to someone who can ensure that what needs to be done can in fact get done.

Risk escalation

This is the only option open to the risk owner when they arrive at a point where they have done everything in their power to manage a risk, but are still unhappy with the severity and feel that it needs further management or control. This is called risk escalation.

In a business setting risk is normally escalated for one of three reasons:

a. The risk owner is unhappy with the severity of the risk and feels that it is of sufficient magnitude that it requires management at a higher level then s/he works (sometimes known as the 'way above my paygrade line')!
b. The risk owner is equally unhappy, but does not have the authority, budget or other resource s/he requires to manage the risk. This will include where action is required to manage the risk which the owner cannot undertake and cannot direct.
c. The risk has the potential to impact upon other parts of the organisation for which the owner has no responsibility.

Remember way back we discussed transfer of risk and how Tom's boss couldn't simply transfer a risk within her organisation to get things done? Let's see how there is a more effective to ensure that we get things done.

Sketch 7

You will recall that Tom's company has an objective that they will achieve an 80% occupancy rate for all their coach journeys. Tom is very much involved in meeting this target but he has a problem; the transport management system he is using is very unreliable due to the poor connectivity in the garage, and that means he constantly is uncertain what the maintenance state of the coaches is, and as a result can't always be sure that he will be able to provide the coaches required for a job. He knows that if they have to cancel a trip that will have a serious effect on customer confidence and could lead to reduced bookings. As Tom is responsible for ensuring that vehicles are ready when required, he has identified it as a risk, which he articulates thus:

> *There is a risk that we will fail to provide a vehicle for a scheduled trip. This will be caused by an inability to properly plan maintenance schedules due to the poor IT connectivity at the garage and the impact will be that we will suffer reputational damage and loss of income from cancelled trips.*

First of all, can Tom own this risk? On the face of it, as Tom is responsible if the risk occurs then yes, he should be the owner. Tom quickly recognises however that while he can make decisions about the risk, it is not within his gift to turn those decisions into action. He has a couple of options. He can speak to the IT Manager directly and try and get the issue resolved. Depending on the organisation this will often be a good place to start, but Tom would need to be pretty confident that the end result of the conversation would be the problem being fixed without delay, thereby dealing effectively with the risk. But what if Tom doesn't have that confidence? Perhaps the IT Manager tells him he can do it but it will take 6 months because there is no budget, or because he has more pressing priorities, or it may just be that Tom's previous experience suggests that the IT Manager doesn't deliver what he says he will.

The risk won't go away just because Tom has asked the IT department to fix it (remember the discussion about transferring risks earlier on?) If the risk still occurs, Tom is going to be the one held responsible, because his boss could easily say that she didn't know anything about it (unless she is like my boss who would never do that!).

Tom's other option then is to escalate the risk, because he has done all in his power to control it, but he is still not happy and can't make further decisions. Tom decides to escalate the risk to his line manager Sally who is the Logistics Director and sits on the Board. Sally still can't tell the IT Manager to get it done, because the IT manager works for someone else, but she can raise the risk at Board level get buy in from the Team and then the direction goes down to the IT Manager, and hey presto!

In this case then, risk ownership has temporarily transferred to the Logistics Director but it doesn't need to stay there. When she can safely return it to the Transport Manager, which will be once the IT situation is resolved, the risk is said to be de-escalated.

Key points
- *If your risk decision is anything other than tolerate, your target score must be lower than your residual.*
- *Three reasons for escalating*
  - *Severity, when the impacts are just too great*
  - *Scope, when it covers parts of the organisation for which you are not responsible*
  - *Gift, when you don't have the resource to manage it*
- *Once under effective control, if appropriate risks can be de-escalated*

Chapter 9

Risk reporting

Once all these steps have been taken and a risk (or more likely a set of risks) is being managed, then someone somewhere is going to want to see assurance that the risks are indeed being managed and that everything is as it should be.

I am going to touch only lightly on this, because as a risk owner you probably won't have much say in how your risks are reported; that is down to whoever maintains your risk management system, but this usually means taking a report on the risks to a management meeting where they can be reviewed and scrutinised. There are many ways of doing this, but essentially they can be divided into two camps.

- Risk Management Software solutions
- Spreadsheets

Software solutions are as varied as the risks they are used for and can range from simple and relatively cheap solutions, to complex modelling software that can cost tens of thousands of pounds and requires dedicated resources to use.

More commonly however is the development of what is called a risk register, which is essentially a list of all the risks an organisation or part of it holds. These are frequently presented as a humble spreadsheet. Some organisations will display their risk registers live at the meeting where they are required, others will produce printed copies.

It must be remembered with risk registers however, that they are simply a point in time; a snap-shot of what the risk picture was at the time it was produced, and this brings me onto a very important point. The more we computerise systems and the more risk registers we produce, it is sometimes easy to get caught up in the process. But risk registers don't manage risks, and neither does software; People manage risks. Your risk register is nothing more than a visual representation of risk information at a given point in time and is usually produced to make it easier to get a fuller picture of risks in a management meeting or similar forum. But for it to be any real use it must be accurate and the information in it up to date.

You will have to find out which system your organisation uses and then work out how you interact with it. This again is where your risk manager can help you.

A comprehensive risk register will present a visual representation of all the information gathered throughout the course of this book. For this reason they can be a little unwieldy in print and not really practicable to reproduce here.

I have however provided an example of a risk register spreadsheet on my website, which is available free to download and use if you wish. You should note however that if you asked 100 different risk managers for examples, you would probably get 100 different versions. It really boils down to how much information you want to present and how much your senior managers want to see.

The example I give however is simple to use, and just needs to be populated with all the information that you collect in your risk analysis activity.

Conclusion

We tend to ignore or at least minimise risks all the time, after all it used to be said that, ignorance is safety. Or so we thought. It used to be the case that managers could effectively bury their heads in the sand and just pretend a risk didn't exists if it was too uncomfortable. Or they would focus on the problem, because frequently the problem was 'somewhere else'; it was in another department or another office, but it was someone else's 'problem'.

Today's corporate world requires a different attitude towards risk and a new breed of risk owners to come to the fore and take the reins, because a company that doesn't understand and controls it's risks is not going to last long. And managers who don't understand what it means to be a risk owner are going to find their CVs getting longer as their career path lengthens.

If this book achieves one thing of course I would want it to be that you understand what it means to be a risk owner. But perhaps equally important is that you grasp the realisation that there is a difference between risks and problems. Some of you will have got this already, but many still don't get it, and if we are going to improve risk management in organisations we have to get more people on board with this simple concept.

This book has never been intended to provide a comprehensive guide to the study of risk management, there are plenty who have gone before who have done an admirable job of this. Not only that but risk managers in general have a pretty good understanding of risk management, it's just that by the nature of their positions they don't actually do it.

I have worked in a number of organisations where I have run teams of risk managers, but one of the hardest jobs that I have found was persuading people that my managers were there to build and manage the systems, and provide the tools because and it was the job of everyone in the organisation to manage Business Continuity, Risk and Information Governance.

This is why I consider the role of the risk owner to be so important.

A good and effective risk management system depends very much on risk owners engaging with it, and understanding what risk ownership means and how to go about it. As risk owners you will take hold of risks, own them, manage them and help to steer your organisation towards its objectives. It is not and cannot be left in the hands of risk managers, no matter how competent they may be. They cannot do it without your help. To paraphrase the late John F. Kennedy...

> *'Ask not what your risk manager can do for you, ask what you can do for your risk manager'*

In conclusion, what I am saying is don't think because your organisation has a risk manager that you can relax in the knowledge that someone else is doing everything. What is it that keeps you awake at night? What gives you that dry mouth in the management meeting? What makes you drift off and suddenly realise you have missed the last 10 minutes of your favourite TV show? The risk manager can't deal with that; it takes a risk owner – a professional risk owner.

References

As I have mentioned before this was never intended as an academic work, so you will not find Harvard referencing or a full bibliography. I have been inspired and influenced by some great writers, some I have mentioned, many I have not. So I will leave you with a list of books as suggested further reading if you are so inclined.

Enjoy...

The Failure Of Risk Management, Douglas W. Hubbard

How to Measure Anything, Douglas W. Hubbard

The Black Swan, Nicholas Nasim Taleb

Fooled by Randomness, Nicholas Nasim Taleb

Thinking Fast and Slow, Daniel Kahneman

Against the Gods; the remarkable story of risk, Peter Bernstein

Blackbox Thinking, Matthew Syed

Printed in Great Britain
by Amazon

80610894R00046